newp

D1050035

/0/ / /

174

YOU CHOOSE™
BOOKS

BUILDING THE
Great Wall
OF CHINA

An Interactive Engineering Adventure

by Allison Lassieur

Consultant:
Hanchao Lu, PhD
Professor of History
Georgia Institute of Technology

CAPSTONE PRESS
a capstone imprint

You Choose Books are published by Capstone Press,
1710 Roe Crest Drive, North Mankato, Minnesota 56003
www.capstonepub.com

B+T 31.99 10/17

Library of Congress Cataloging-in-Publication Data
Lassieur, Allison.
  Building the Great Wall of China : an interactive engineering adventure / by Allison Lassieur.
      pages cm—(You choose. Engineering marvels)
  Includes bibliographical references and index.
  Summary: "Explores various perspectives on the process of building the Great Wall of China. The
reader's choices reveal the historical details"—Provided by publisher.
  ISBN 978-1-4914-0399-0 (library binding)
  ISBN 978-1-4914-0404-1 (paperback)
  ISBN 978-1-4914-0408-9 (ebook PDF)
1. Great Wall of China (China)—Juvenile literature. I. Title.
  DS793.G67L37 2015
  951—dc23   2013047365

Editorial Credits
Adrian Vigliano, editor; Veronica Scott, designer; Wanda Winch, media researcher; Laura Manthe,
production specialist

Photo Credits
Bridgeman Art Library: © Look and Learn/Private Collection, cover, 38, 84, © Look and Learn/
Private Collection/C.L. Doughty, 88, © Look and Learn/Private Collection/Pat Nicolle, 65, Royal
Geographical Society, London, UK/Herbert Ponting, 100; Capstone, 23; Corbis: Dean Conger,
105; Dreamstime: Bjmcse, 99; Getty Images Inc: The Bridgeman Art Library, 66, The Bridgeman
Art Library/Angus McBride, 92, The British Library/Robana, 10, China Photos, 58, DEA Picture
Library, 80, Gallo Images/Travel Ink, 45, National Geographic/Lloyd Kenneth Townsend, Jr., 29;
TAO Images Limited, 48, UIG/SOVfoto, 12; Newscom: ViewStock Stock Connection, USA, 6;
Osprey Publishing: "The Great Wall of China 221 BC-AD 1644", 52; Shutterstock: alekup, grunge
blueprint design, axz700, 74, Hung Chung Chih, cover (inset), lapas77, 16, Sociologas, graph paper
design; Wikipedia: GruDoyng, 70

Printed in Canada.
032014   008086FRF14

TABLE OF CONTENTS

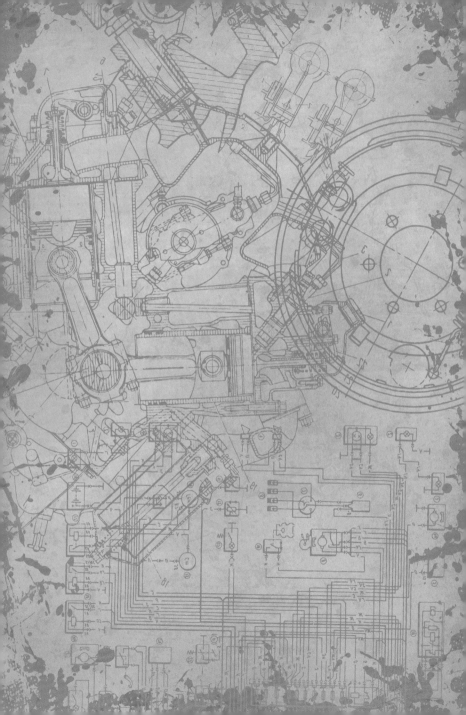

About Your Adventure

The Great Wall of China is one of the most impressive structures ever built. From the earliest walls to the grand towers and fortresses, the Great Wall is a symbol of China and its people.

In this book you'll explore how the choices people made meant the difference between life and death. The events you'll experience happened to real people.

Chapter One sets the scene. Then you choose which path to read. Follow the directions at the bottom of each page. The choices you make will change your outcome. After you finish one path, go back and read the others for new perspectives and more adventures.

*YOU CHOOSE the path
you take through history.*

The Great Wall of China is the longest structure human beings have ever built.

THE LONGEST WALL IN THE WORLD

The Great Wall of China has been a part of your life since you were born. It is as ancient as the land and as strong as the most terrible dragon. The wall stretches across the land and disappears over the mountains. You feel proud as you look at it. Your ancestors helped to build the first earthen walls in 221 BC. The First Emperor, Qin Shi Huang, ordered that the first part of the Great Wall be built. But Emperor Qin Shi Huang's wall wasn't the first wall in China.

7

Turn the page.

Before Emperor Qin Shi Huang, China was filled with villages and small cities. It was hard to defend them against attacking enemies. One way that villagers protected their homes was by building walls. Qin Shi Huang was the first person to unify all the villages and cities into one empire. He liked the idea of protective walls, so he ordered that the walls be joined into one long wall. Thousands of soldiers, farmers, and prisoners built these new walls. For a time, the walls worked. But the First Emperor fell ill and died in 210 BC, and wall building stopped.

Later emperors kept building and improving the wall, hoping to keep out the invaders. The wall helped in defending China, but invaders continued to mount attacks. Some of your other ancestors fought China's enemies along the wall.

The wall you know was built during the Ming Dynasty, from AD 1368 to 1644. Thousands of miles of walls, forts, castles, towers, and battlements were added. Workers built every inch of the wall out of earth, brick, and stone. The wall snaked through deserts and forests and wound along mountaintops. The farmers in your family grew the food that fed the builders.

Turn the page.

秦始皇

姓嬴名政始自皇帝乙卯即王位庚辰併天下稱皇帝
在位三十七年居王位二十五年即帝位十二年壽五十

Qin Shi Huang chose to rule as an emperor,
rather than using the king title of the rulers
who came before him.

By the 1600s China was no longer at war. The Great Wall was left to ruin. People took the bricks and stone from the crumbling walls to build their own homes. Large sections of the wall disappeared. In some areas people forgot the wall had ever existed.

But others did not forget. The Great Wall is filled with the stories of the people who built it. Every stone is wet with the tears of the workers who suffered. Every brick is covered with the blood of those who died. The towers and battlements still ring with the sounds of war.

To be a peasant forced to work on the First Emperor's wall, turn to page 13.

To be a bricklayer working on the wall during the Ming Dynasty, turn to page 39.

To be an architect who designs the Ming towers and battlements, turn to page 67.

A beacon tower sits alongside a trench in northwestern China. It marks an ancient portion of the Great Wall.

CHAPTER 2

THE FIRST WALLS GO UP

The cold room you are locked in smells like sweat and human filth. Something red has stained the thin walls. Blood, probably. Maybe your father was held here when he was arrested years ago. That was in 219 BC, when you were a child. He was a peasant farmer. The emperor's men took him away and you never saw him again.

You blame the emperor for all of this. Not that long ago, China was at war with itself. Seven different states fought one another for power. In 221 BC all the states came together under the First Emperor Qin Shi Huang. Emperor Qin is a cruel ruler. He believes that human nature is basically bad. People should be punished harshly for any bad thing they do.

Turn the page.

You have no idea why you are here, but it was probably because of someone else. Every family in your village is registered with the government. Your family is part of a bigger group of other families in the village. Every family in the group is responsible for the other families. If one person breaks the law, everyone in the group is punished for it.

Two guards burst into the small room.

"You are lucky today," one of them says. "The emperor himself is in the village. He will punish you and the rest of the dirty peasants himself."

"Maybe he'll have your nose and feet cut off," the other guard says.

"He might have you branded. Or you could be boiled alive. You are as good as dead."

The door is wide open, and you are small and fast.

To escape, go to page 15.

To stay, turn to page 17.

Don't look back, you think as you race through the door. The dense forest beyond the village will be a great place to hide. The guards are right behind you. You run into the forest. Soon you don't hear the guards behind you anymore. You crawl under a fallen tree and hide until dark.

It's colder and darker than you thought. As the night wears on, your stomach growls. You wish you had been able to grab some food or a blanket. You briefly consider going back to the village to gather some supplies. But you realize it might be easier to try to get to the next village.

15

Turn the page.

It's only a few miles to the next village and you know the way. Ignoring the cold, you find the road and set out. You are so focused on your misery that you don't hear the hoofbeats behind you until it's too late. The guards grab you, tie your hands, and throw you over the back of a horse. You're so cold and hungry that you don't even care.

In 1974 farmers discovered thousands of clay warriors buried around Emperor Qin Shi Huang's tomb. This army includes more than 8,000 life-size soldiers and other figures. Historians think this terra-cotta army was made to protect the emperor's tomb in the afterlife.

Soon you are standing in front of the emperor. Crowds of villagers watch silently as the emperor stares at you.

"Do you know what they say about me?" he asks. "I have the heart of a wolf and I show little mercy. But I will show mercy today and spare you and your family."

Relief floods through you. The emperor continues. "A dead peasant is a useless peasant. I need workers on a big project. It is the Long Wall of Ten Thousand Li."

17

Turn the page.

You have heard terrible stories of the wall. When Emperor Qin unified China, several small walls snaked through China. They protected the lands of the different tribes. The emperor wanted to join these small walls into one long wall. He wanted to protect his new empire from his enemies. Tens of thousands of people have been forced to work on the Long Wall. Many of them have never come back.

"Your sentence is four years of hard labor," the emperor says. "In my mercy, I will let you choose. You can work on the wall. Or you can work in the food caravans that deliver food to the workers."

To work on the Long Wall, go to page 19.

To work as a food caravan driver, turn to page 26.

For days you and the other prisoners are forced to march through the wilderness to the wall. The days become a blur of exhaustion, hunger, and thirst. At night everyone sleeps on the ground, even in the rain. The only thing you get to eat is one small bowl of food a day.

Late one night you wake up to go to the toilet. Everything is quiet. Even the guards are asleep. If you want to escape, now is the time. You're not sure where you are. You could die in the woods alone. But you could die on this terrible march too.

19

To stay and continue on, turn to page 20.

To take your chances in the wilderness, turn to page 28.

The terrible march goes on for another week. The land becomes rough, with steep, rocky hills. But you manage to make it. Finally you see the construction site. A giant wall twists up and down along the tops of the hills. Parts of the wall are half finished. Thousands of workers swarm everywhere. Some are bent with the weight of heavy baskets. Others push carts full of earth and rock. Lines of people stand on the half-completed wall, tramping the earth.

"Are they all prisoners?" you gasp.

The guard laughs. "No. Most of the workers are soldiers or common peasants. They are forced to work just like you are. In fact, every male over 4 feet tall is forced to work on the Long Wall. That means some of the workers are children. The rest are prisoners."

A tall man in military clothing speaks to the guard. He turns and says, "I am General Meng Tian. My task is building the Long Wall."

He points to the construction. "The Long Wall is built from earth and any other materials we can find in the area," he says. "First the workers build a wall-shaped frame out of wood or bamboo. Other workers fill the frame with earth and other materials. They stand on top of the earth and tamp it down to make it hard and tight. Then workers put another layer of earth on top and tamp it again. They keep doing this until the wall is about 20 feet high."

"I need workers to dig and carry earth and rocks to the wall," Meng says. "I also need workers to build frames and tamp the earth."

To dig earth and rocks and carry them, turn to page 22.

To tamp earth, turn to page 23.

To build frames, turn to page 25.

The march here was nothing compared to the work of building the wall. There is hardly anything to eat. The workers begin at dawn and work until dark. They tell you horrible stories of how the emperor's soldiers took them away from their homes. Some of them haven't seen their families in years.

At night you sleep with the others in makeshift camps near the wall. The hard, cold ground is your bed. There are no blankets or tents. Everyone sleeps outside, no matter what the weather. You only get enough food to survive. Every day workers die of starvation and sickness. Their bodies are buried in huge ditches that run along the wall.

Today you can work carrying earth for the wall. Or you can dig rocks from a nearby quarry.

22

To carry earth, turn to page 29.

To work at the quarry, turn to page 31.

You join the workers along the wall. Workers bring basketfuls of earth and clay and pour them on the top of the wall. You drop a large, heavy tool onto the dirt to pack it down.

Workers use heavy tools to tamp, or pack down the wall's dirt surface. This process helped strengthen the wall.

Turn the page.

It takes hours to build up only a few inches of earth wall. When you are done, workers build the frame a little higher. Once the wall is about 20 feet high, you will start working on the next section.

Some people say that the bodies of dead workers are buried in the wall. You've never seen a body buried there, but you would not be surprised. Already, people are calling the wall the "World's Longest Cemetery."

Eventually this section of the wall is done. You can keep tamping earth, or you can help build the wooden frame for the next section.

24

To build the frames, go to page 25.

To stay on the wall, turn to page 36.

Frame building is hard but not as terrible as the tasks some other workers have to do. Your grandfather was a woodworker and he taught you well.

Today you are building frames out of wood from the nearby forest. Sometimes the frames are made out of bamboo. It all depends on what is available nearby. You do your best to make the frame sturdy. The other workers don't have your skill, and they don't seem to care about building a strong frame.

When it is done the frame is not as sturdy as you'd like. You are worried that it isn't going to hold the weight of the earth, rocks, and workers. If you tell a soldier you might be punished or killed. But if you don't tell anyone and the frame fails, the same thing could happen.

25

To stay quiet, turn to page 33.

To alert a soldier, turn to page 34.

Four years driving a cart filled with food doesn't seem so bad. But the job turns out to be worse than you thought. The trip to the construction site takes many days. You are punished if you do not deliver the food on time. But the worst problem is the bandits. They attack caravans and steal the food. There should be soldiers along the roads to protect the caravans. You rarely see one, though.

You heard a story about the bandits and caravans. A caravan of almost 200 carts of grain once set out for the Long Wall. Only one cart arrived safely. Many workers starved to death when the food did not come.

In only two more days you will be at the Long Wall again. Suddenly a group bursts out of the trees beside the road. The bandits crowd around, digging through the cart to see what food you have. One pulls you off the cart and throws you onto the muddy ground.

Most of the time bandits leave you alone and take the food. Not today. The leader pulls out a knife and shoves it into your stomach. The last thing you hear is their laugher as you fall, your blood turning the mud red as you die.

THE END

To follow another path, turn to page 11.
To read the conclusion, turn to page 101.

You disappear into the woods and run until you can't move. At dawn you crawl under a fallen tree and sleep. When you wake up, the sun has set. No one seems to have come looking for you.

You feel lucky when you find a small stream of cold, fresh water. You follow it for several days until a small village appears through the trees. You stumble into the village and pass out in the dirt.

When you wake up, you're comfortable and warm. Someone feeds you hot soup. Slowly you tell the villagers your terrible story. They don't seem shocked. They know about the prisoners and the marches to the Long Wall. They promise to help you get back to your village when you are stronger. But for now, it is enough that you have survived.

28

THE END

To follow another path, turn to page 11.
To read the conclusion, turn to page 101.

You strap a large basket on your back and make the day's first trip to the digging area. A digger fills your basket with earth. The first few loads are not too bad. But they seem to get heavier as the day wears on. Over and over you walk the path, bent in pain. The hours blend into one long day of agony.

The Great Wall project required the work of a huge number of soldiers, common people, and criminals.

Turn the page.

When the sun goes down, you make it to camp and crumple onto the ground. The next morning the call comes to wake up, but you can't move. Each of your muscles screams in pain. As you struggle to stand you realize that you must have injured your back as well. The previous day's work pushed your body too far. Guards come and haul you to your feet, but you collapse.

For several days you lay there, moaning, and everyone ignores you. Then one morning you wake up with a fever and a terrible cough. Throughout the day you feel your remaining strength disappear. As you slowly slip into unconsciousness, you feel thankful that the pain is gone. You will probably be another body in the ditch by morning, but you don't care anymore.

THE END

To follow another path, turn to page 11.
To read the conclusion, turn to page 101.

Hundreds of workers are already at the quarry when you arrive. To save money and time, each section of the Long Wall is built with whatever materials are on hand. This is a rocky, hilly area, so rocks go into the Long Wall.

Soon you're filling basket after basket with rocks. Suddenly one of the workers slips and falls to the bottom of the quarry, hitting several rocky ledges on his way down. Soldiers come and take away his lifeless body. Someone else steps forward, and you fill his basket. You wonder if the dead worker had family somewhere. If so, they will probably never know what happened to him. When the sun goes down you head back to camp.

Turn the page.

As you try to fall asleep, you think about the dead worker. You remember a poem another prisoner recited to you. It is about all the people who have died building the Long Wall. It goes,

> "If you have a son, don't raise him.
> If you have a girl, feed her dried meat.
> Can't you see the Long Wall
> Is propped up by skeletons."

The next day you take extra care, remembering what happened the day before. Around noon you kneel at the quarry edge to fill your basket with rocks. Suddenly the ground begins to crumble under your feet. The quarry edge collapses, sending you down toward the rocks below. Before you have a chance to react, your head slams into something hard and everything goes black.

THE END

To follow another path, turn to page 11.
To read the conclusion, turn to page 101.

Speaking up isn't worth your life. The soldiers send you to a different part of the site to build another frame. Soon you're so focused on the work that you forget your concerns.

Around mid-afternoon everyone is startled by a huge crash. The frame you were worried about has collapsed into a heap of splintered wood. Two workers fell, screaming, on top of the sharp wood. All of the earth that had been tamped that morning has now crumbled away.

The soldiers grab you and the other workers who built the collapsed frame. They haul you before General Meng Tian. He says only one word. "Death." You are taken to the edge of the burial pit. The last sight you see in this life is the corpses of all the dead workers in twisted heaps below you.

THE END

To follow another path, turn to page 11.
To read the conclusion, turn to page 101.

You find a soldier and tell him the problem. The soldier gives the frame a hard shake. A section pulls away and crashes to the ground. Without a word the soldier grabs your arm and drags you toward the soldiers' camp.

General Meng Tian sees you coming. The soldier explains what happened as you bow your head in fear. The general is silent for so long that finally you look up.

"I do not understand why you would do such a terrible job, then confess to it," he says. "Do you want to die?"

Quickly you explain. The general considers your words. "So, you have some skill with building," he says. "Can you teach others how to build?"

"Yes," you say.

"Then go to the supervisor and tell him I want you to begin in the morning." The general turns away and doesn't give you another thought.

Before you know it you are in another camp. You have a small tent, a blanket, and some hot food. In the morning you will teach others how to build properly.

You continue teaching for 6 years. Because of your good work, the general lets you go back your village. You are happy to be back with your family.

THE END

To follow another path, turn to page 11.
To read the conclusion, turn to page 101.

Day after day you tamp earth with the others. One section of wall takes many days to finish. Slowly the wall rises. It snakes along the top of a high ridge overlooking vast forests. You hear that the wall will protect the new empire from outside enemies. You don't know why the emperor needs a wall in such a remote area. Some workers whisper that the emperor's mind is leaving him.

So many people die every day that you cannot count the bodies. They make you think of the legend of Meng Jiangnu. Meng's husband was sent to work on the Long Wall. He did not come home before winter set in. Meng was worried that her husband would be cold, so she took some warm clothes to the Long Wall for him. When she got there, she could not find him. Finally someone told her that he had died. Meng Jiangnu cried for many days. Her tears split open the Long Wall. Inside the earth she found the bones of her husband and all the others who had died building the Long Wall. She buried her husband's bones and then killed herself.

Four years pass. The day you are set free, you weep. You think of your family, hoping they will still be there to greet you when you return.

THE END

To follow another path, turn to page 11.
To read the conclusion, turn to page 101.

Most wall construction during the Ming Dynasty used bricks and mortar as the main building materials.

CHAPTER 3

BUILDING THE WALL, BRICK BY BRICK

The Ming Emperor's soldiers came to your village in the night. They were looking for people to work on the emperor's grand project: The Great Wall.

You have heard about the wall all your life. Many centuries ago the First Emperor built a Long Wall to protect the land. Your parents told you stories about the Long Wall. You, like many others, weren't sure the Long Wall really existed.

Today the soldiers have changed everyone's mind. The First Ming emperor, Hongwu, and the Chinese army drove the Mongols out of China in 1368. The Ming Dynasty began. Since then war has torn the land. Mongol invaders and other nomads keep attacking.

Turn the page.

To protect China Hongwu started rebuilding the wall. He decided that the only way to stop them was to rebuild and repair the old walls to keep them out. Since then other Ming emperors have kept up the building. The Ming walls must be bigger and stronger than the ancient wall of the First Emperor. That is why the soldiers are here.

The soldiers are especially in need of skilled workers like you. They are asking thousands of farmers, architects, stonecutters, brick makers, and other workers to move to the construction site. The men in your family have been brick makers for many generations. The soldiers want to make you a deal: you won't have to pay any taxes if you agree to work. You will be paid for your work. They also say you will be able to come home after a few months.

To stay in your home village, go to page 41.

To agree to go work on the walls, turn to page 42.

The soldiers leave without you. You are shocked that they didn't force you to go with them. It may be because you are not a criminal. The emperor punishes some criminals by forcing them to work on the wall for their whole lives. But it is worse than that. If the criminal dies while working on the wall, one of his relatives must work in his place.

For a time you forget about the wall. Then one day the village is filled with rumors of soldiers in the countryside, looking for recruits again. They might not bother you this time. But if they do come, you might not be lucky again. No one says no to the soldiers twice and lives.

To leave your village, turn to page 54.

To stay, turn to page 55.

It will take many days to get to the construction site, but you are not worried. The road winds through beautiful countryside, and the first few days are bright and clear. But by the end of the week, the rains come. Everyone is wet and miserable. A few people become ill with fever and chills. The whole group slows down for the weakened people. After a while, some of the healthy people want to ride on and leave the sick ones behind. You can go with them. But maybe you should stay and help take care of the sick.

42

To ride on, go to page 43.

To stay, turn to page 56.

After a few days the rains stop, and the rest of the trip is warm and comfortable. You tell stories to pass the time, including a brick-making story your father told you about the Great Wall.

"There is a place," you begin, "where the wall was built on the spine of a mountain. It was too steep to carry stone and brick up the mountain. And there was no flat place nearby for brick kilns. The overseer did not know what to do. A local man named Li Gang offered to make bricks several miles away. But when the bricks were made, Li Gang did not know how to get them up the mountain."

43

Turn the page.

"Li Gang took a nap," you continue, "and dreamed of a magical ox that could carry the bricks. In the dream the ox carried tens of thousands of bricks up the mountain. When Li Gang woke up, he was shocked to see that all of his bricks were really gone! Quickly he went to the mountain. There he saw that all the bricks he made had been built into the Great Wall."

Finally your group arrives at the wall. The supervisor in charge of construction is happy to see you. He needs brick makers to go to the brick-making workshop. It is about a mile away from the main construction site. He also needs bricklayers to go to the construction site immediately.

To go to the brick-making workshop, go to page 45.

To start laying bricks on the Great Wall, turn to page 50.

Around the workshop the air is choked with smoke from the dozens of kilns that fill this flat area. An endless sea of tree stumps and brush stretches as far as you can see. Thousands of people swarm in the workshop. To unskilled workers this might look like a disorganized mess. But you can see that the work is very organized.

Kilns are ovenlike chambers used to capture heat and control temperature. They are essential in the process of traditional brick-making.

Turn the page.

Workers dig the earth for the bricks in areas away from the construction site. Another group of workers molds the earth into brick shapes and bakes them in the kilns until they are hard.

The brick makers are using three different kinds of kilns. One design looks like a dragon, with several ovens for firing the bricks. Another kiln is U-shaped, and the third is shaped like a horn.

Near the kilns workers pull finished bricks from the ovens. The bricks get stacked in piles or neat rows. Other workers are carrying wood and other fuels for the kilns. Even more men dig earth to make clay and fill molds. Lines of workers fill baskets and carts with bricks to carry to the construction site.

You're not sure where to start.

To gather fuel, go to page 47.

To make the clay and fill the molds, turn to page 48.

To fire the bricks in the kilns, turn to page 58.

It takes a lot of fuel to build the fires to make bricks. The only job that many workers have is gathering fuel for the kilns. The best fire for the bricks comes from layers of grass, a type of wood called wormwood, and pine branches. Sometimes it is better to use heavy oil and sheep or goat dung. These fuels make the fire smokier. The smoke makes the bricks stronger.

There is a lot of good fuel in this area. Some workers cut down trees while others gather pine branches. When you have filled your basket, you go back to the main brick-making workshop and decide you're ready for a new challenge.

47

To make clay and fill molds, turn to page 48.
To fire bricks in the kilns, turn to page 58.

Some workers dig the earth and clay that will be used to make bricks. They fill carts and baskets with earth from a huge pit. Others cut large pieces of earth and grass and pile them on the carts. Earth with grass roots in it makes strong bricks. Workers bring buckets of water to mix in the earth to make a thick mud.

Some bricks in the Great Wall are stamped with information about who made them.

A large area around the workshop is covered with square wooden molds. Each mold is the size of one brick. Every brick will be about 14 inches long, 7 inches deep, and 4 inches wide.

You and the others pour the thick mud into the wooden molds, and then press the mud down. When the bricks are dry, they will be fired in the kilns. You could wait for the bricks to dry, but you don't want to be accused of not working hard enough. Perhaps it would be better to help the diggers while you wait.

49

To dig earth, turn to page 57.

To rest and wait for the bricks to dry, turn to page 58.

After a hard climb, you arrive at the construction area. The size of the wall takes your breath away. It twists up and down the mountain like a dragon and disappears in the distance. Square watchtowers sit at different points on the wall. Small villages dot the valley far below.

It's hard to breathe through the thick smoke and smell of fires and human waste. A sea of tree stumps and mud stretches out from both sides of the wall. The air is filled with the sounds of hammering and shouting. Carts filled with building materials crisscross the construction site. Lines of workers trudge along the wall with their loads.

A sweaty man appears. "I am the overseer of the bricklaying," he says. "I need some men to work on the outer brick 'skin' of the wall, and others for bricklaying jobs on the top of the wall."

To work on the top of the wall, go to page 51.

To work on the outer section of the wall, turn to page 60.

You climb steep stairs to the top. The stairs are only on the China side of the wall. On the other side, there is nothing but wall. You see a long line of workers stretching up the mountain. They pass baskets and bricks from one person to the next, up the slope.

The top of the wall is crawling with workers. A supervisor sees you. "Good, more workers!" he exclaims. When you tell him you are a master bricklayer, he grins. "Just what I need," he says.

He shows you around. "See how wide the top of the wall is?" he asks. "It must be wide enough for five horsemen to gallop side by side, or ten soldiers to march in a row. It is called the 'horse road wall.'"

51

The supervisor needs people to lay bricks on the walkway. He could also use people to mix the mortar that holds the bricks together.

To work on the wide walkway, turn to page 52.

To mix mortar, turn to page 62.

Laying bricks is especially tricky here. The bricks must be of the best quality. The walkway must slope gently outward to let the rain drain away. And the whole walkway must be so well laid that it is watertight. You're good at your job, so this is no problem.

Building a strong wall on sloped ground required great architectural skill.

Every day you rise at dawn and climb the steep stairs to the top of the wall. Even though you are a faceless, nameless worker, you take pride in your job. Every brick must be laid perfectly. When it rains, the water drains exactly as it should.

The supervisor notices your good work. He shows you a different part of the wall. "See these open spaces in the wall? They are *duo-kou*, or battlements. Soldiers use the openings to watch for barbarians or shoot them with arrows."

He gives you the choice of working on the battlements or installing drain spouts along the wall.

53

To work on the battlements, turn to page 63.

To install drain spouts, turn to page 64.

Quickly you tell your family to gather what they can and load it onto your cart. By nightfall you are far away. If the soldiers don't follow you or see you on the road, you might be able to escape.

You travel for many weeks, hoping that your wife's family will take you in—if you are lucky enough to get there. You are thankful for each day of travel that passes without an encounter with soldiers or bandits.

After a two-month journey you arrive at your wife's home village. Her family agrees to give you shelter. You thank them, promising to repay them one day for their kindness. You hug your family and smile, hoping that you've put the Great Wall behind you forever.

54

THE END

To follow another path, turn to page 11.
To read the conclusion, turn to page 101.

The rumors are true. Another soldier comes looking for you. You tell him you will not go to the wall. You're ready to die when he says something shocking. He doesn't want to take you away!

He wants you to make bricks for the construction. It doesn't matter that you live miles away from the construction. The soldier makes arrangements to send the finished bricks to the construction site. He gives you money and tells you to get to work. It looks like you will have plenty of work, and money, for many months to come.

THE END

To follow another path, turn to page 11.
To read the conclusion, turn to page 101.

At first people seem to be getting well. Then one by one they start to get worse. Some die, and no one knows why. You decide to continue taking care of them and hope you don't get sick too.

One morning you awake with a terrible headache and fever. Your muscles ache and you feel cold. It becomes hard to breathe and you know your luck has run out. You slip into unconsciousness like many others, and die of this mysterious illness.

THE END

To follow another path, turn to page 11.
To read the conclusion, turn to page 101.

Not wanting to take any changes, you decide to help the diggers make the mud clay for the bricks. Later a building supervisor appears. He is furious! He says that the last batch of bricks was bad. He rounds up everyone who worked on that batch. You try to explain that you are a brick maker, just helping out the diggers. But he doesn't listen. One by one you are all killed for the mistake.

THE END

To follow another path, turn to page 11.
To read the conclusion, turn to page 101.

You decide to stick with the bricks and no one pays you any mind. Once the bricks are dry you stack them by rows into the kiln to be fired. Each kiln can hold 5,000 bricks, and you pack it full. It takes seven days to fire a kiln full of bricks. You stack the bricks on the first day. The next day you fire them. The third day you pour water on top of the kiln to help cool down the bricks.

Modern Chinese workers use traditional methods to make kiln-fired bricks.

You let the bricks cool for the next three days. On the seventh day, workers unload the kiln. Brand-new bricks are ready to go to the Great Wall. Most of the bricks are plain. You stamp your name in some of them.

Each day you and the other brick makers move from one kiln to the next, doing whatever job needs to be done. One day you are getting a stack of fuel ready for firing. When you light the fire, a gust of wind takes you by surprise. Sparks fly into your clothing and burst into flames! You run, screaming, until someone throws water onto your burning clothes. The burns cover most of your body. After a few days in agony, you die from your injuries.

THE END

To follow another path, turn to page 11.
To read the conclusion, turn to page 101.

Large sections of the wall are only half finished. In some sections workers push huge, heavy blocks of stone into place to make a foundation. In another area, workers build the inside of the wall by tamping down earth. When the earthen wall is tall enough, bricklayers build a brick "skin" over it for strength. Other workers add stones to parts of the wall.

The bricklayers in this section work on scaffolding about halfway up the wall. You climb up a ladder and start working. You stop when the sun goes down. At dawn the next day, you start working again.

Weeks pass. The wall goes up slowly. The building supervisors are unhappy with the slow pace. Every day they shout to go faster. The emperor wants the wall finished, they say. More bricklayers arrive and climb the scaffolding. One day a huge cracking sound splits the air. The scaffolding collapses under the weight of the extra workers. Everyone crashes to the ground in a heap of splintered wood and broken bodies. You and the other dead workers are quickly buried in ditches alongside the wall.

THE END

To follow another path, turn to page 11.
To read the conclusion, turn to page 101.

The mortar in the large tubs looks strange and white. You have never seen white mortar before. Another worker laughs when you ask about it.

"We make special mortar with lime, clay, and white sticky rice soup!" he says. "The sticky rice mortar is so strong that weeds do not grow through. The emperor has ordered that all the rice grown in southern China go to making mortar and to feeding the workers." You smile, happy at the thought of food. But then you wonder if the people in southern China will be hungry this winter.

You mix the sticky rice mortar all day. The next day the supervisor finds you. The mortar you mixed the day before wasn't right. He doesn't have time for people who can't do their jobs, he says. He drags you away, and no one ever sees you again.

THE END

To follow another path, turn to page 11.
To read the conclusion, turn to page 101.

You're an expert at building straight, strong walls. But these battlements are different than what you've worked on in the past. The bricks are not laid in straight, flat lines. They are sloped to the angle of the land. The workers explain that this method allows them to build faster because they don't have to make sure every brick is level. It seems strange to you, but you start working. To your surprise the brick laying does go faster using the sloped building method.

Day after day you build the wall. Weeks turn into months, and the building goes on in all kinds of weather. You forget how much time has passed until one day the supervisor appears. He tells you that your time on the wall is over. Finally you can go home.

THE END

To follow another path, turn to page 11.
To read the conclusion, turn to page 101.

The wall's drainage system is simple. Water drains from the walkway through holes in the walls. The water flows into large stone spouts. This system is meant to keep the wall from washing away. The spouts are only on the Chinese side of the wall. This helps prevent plants and trees from growing on the enemy's side, so they won't have any place to hide or get over the wall.

Each spout is cut from one big stone slab. It takes many men to put a spout into the wall. You and the others work on scaffolding high on the wall. Slowly you push the stone spout into place. Suddenly someone slips. The giant stone spout crashes down on you, destroying the scaffolding and sending everyone to their deaths in the forest below.

THE END

To follow another path, turn to page 11.
To read the conclusion, turn to page 101.

Bricks and other building materials had to be moved by laborers. Baskets were one tool workers used to help move materials up and down the wall.

大明太祖高皇帝

Zhu Yuanzhang began life as a poor peasant. He later became the commander of an army that drove out the Mongol rulers of the Yuan Dynasty. He then established the Ming Dynasty and became its first emperor.

CHAPTER 4

THE GREAT MING WALL

You have lived in the shadow of the Great Wall all your life. In the early years of the Ming Dynasty, your ancestors helped to rebuild many ancient sections of the wall that had fallen into ruin. Now it is your turn.

The great Ming Dynasty began in 1368 when Zhu Yuanzhang defeated his rivals at the end of the Mongol-ruled Yuan Dynasty and became the first Ming emperor. He was a strong and ruthless warrior, but the emperors that came after him were not.

67

Many times the Mongols and other enemies defeated the Chinese armies. The Mongols were a constant threat, and no one knew what to do about them. The Chinese armies could not completely defeat them. The Ming rulers didn't want to make friends with them, either. The only thing the Ming rulers could think of to do was to build new walls to keep them out.

The Ming walls include some old walls and many new ones. It is 1568, and the Ming Dynasty has been working on the wall now for more than 200 years. But there is more to be built! Everything will be bigger and stronger than anyone can imagine. The Ming Emperor Longqing has ordered beacon towers, watchtowers, and forts to be designed and built along the wall. He hopes the strength of the wall will keep out all the Mongol enemies.

It is not one single long wall, though. It is known as the "Nine Frontier Garrisons." The wall is divided into nine military districts. Each district has a military garrison and a commander who is in charge of it. Each commander is also in charge of building and maintaining the wall in his garrison.

You are a new architect, still learning how to design buildings. You have been chosen to help with the design of some of the structures. This means that you must leave your wife and child behind in the village. You will miss them terribly. But this is a great chance for you. After weeks of travel you arrive at the construction site. Before you have a chance to get your bearings, a soldier informs you that architects are needed on the watchtowers.

Turn the page.

Older parts of the wall already have towers, but they are little more than earthen platforms where soldiers stand guard. A military commander, Qi Jiguang, wants to build a new kind of tower. He is a garrison commander, and the emperor put him in charge of designing new walls and fortifications.

Qi Jiguang defeated Japanese pirates and Mongol invaders before his assignment on the Great Wall. Many carvings and statues have been made of this Chinese military hero.

When Qi Jiguang first saw the wall, he was unhappy. Many parts of the wall were in ruins. The soldiers had no shelter from the weather. They had to stand in the snow and rain. There weren't any storage areas for weapons or food. And worst of all, the wall was hard to defend from enemies. Now Qi Jiguang is overseeing the construction of new towers, and you are going to work with him.

"We must build better towers," he says when you meet him. "They must be large enough to hold soldiers and supplies. They must also be strong enough to keep our enemies out." Some of towers will be solid with a platform on the top. There will also be hollow towers with rooms and storage areas inside. He gives you the choice between designing a hollow tower and planning the interior space of the towers.

To design a hollow tower, turn to page 72.

To work on the interior space design, turn to page 73.

Qi Jiguang says that each tower must be large enough to house between 30 and 50 men. There must be areas to store weapons. And there must be a place for soldiers to fight and defend the wall. The design you come up with has all of these elements. Your design is approved and the construction starts.

Each tower will be square or rectangular. Each tower is built on top of the wall. The walkway along the top of the wall serves as the tower's floor. The sides of each tower extend out from the wall to give it more space inside. Workers build each tower with two sections. The lower section is for storing weapons. It has windows and openings for soldiers to shoot arrows and cannons at enemies. The top has a high battlement where soldiers can shoot more arrows.

Qi Jiguang is pleased with your design and asks you to choose your next project.

To work on the barracks and storage design, go to page 73.

To design a solid tower, turn to page 94.

To work on the battlements, turn to page 96.

It is important that the soldiers have a warm, dry place to eat and sleep. Each tower has an area where the soldiers can have a meal and relax when they are off duty. You design sleeping platforms heated with coal fires. Now the soldiers will be warm when they sleep. The storage areas are near the barracks. When the enemy attacks, it will be easy for soldiers to get their weapons. Some of the towers are bigger. They will be able to house 100 soldiers and all their supplies.

Qi Jiguang is pleased with your work. "I need a good designer to go to Jiayuguan Pass," he says. "You have the skill to make important repairs to the fort and buildings there."

Jiayuguan Pass is at the far western end of the wall. If you go there you will surely never see your family again. But refusing Qi Jiguang would be a disgrace.

To go to Jiayuguan Pass, turn to page 74.

To respectfully ask to stay here, turn to page 92.

It takes many days of travel to get to Jiayuguan Pass. You gasp when you see the enormous complex and its grand temples and towers. The Ming emperors ordered Jiayuguan Pass built in 1372. It sits near a great desert, and you have no idea what lies beyond the endless sand. The Ming armies use passes through the wall to attack enemies on the other side. Traders also use the passes to come and go through the wall.

Jiayuguan Pass is sometimes called the "First and Greatest Pass Under Heaven." It is one of the largest remaining ancient military castles on the Great Wall.

As you enter Jiayuguan Pass you marvel at the size of the complex. Soldiers, traders, monks, politicians, and townspeople crowd inside the walls. Delicious smells come from the food stalls, but the streets stink with animal dung and human sweat. The complex has three main areas. Most of the buildings are in the inner city, which is about 6 acres wide. The outer city area includes walls, towers, and buildings. Outside that, a moat protects the whole pass from attack.

There are many repairs to do here. You can begin with restoring part of the brick tower. Or you could work on another project in the pass.

To work on the tower, turn to page 76.

To work on other projects, turn to page 78.

The buildings and towers in the complex are hundreds of years old and need constant repair. You are high up on a ladder, replacing some crumbling bricks, when you see something strange. A single brick is out in the open on a tower ledge. Then you remember a legend you heard on the journey here. According to the legend, a man named Yi Kaizhan was helping to build the pass. He was very smart with numbers. He told the overseer that it would take 99,999 bricks to build the Jiayuguan Pass. The overseer didn't believe him. He told Yi Kaizhan that if there were any leftover bricks, he would cut off Yi's head.

When the pass was finished, there was one brick left. The overseer was about to make good on his threat when Yi Kaizhan stopped him.

Yi pointed to that last brick. It was sitting on a ledge on the main tower of the pass. Yi Kaizhan said that a magical god put the leftover brick on the tower. If the brick were moved, he said, the whole pass would collapse. The overseer was afraid to move the brick or kill Yi Kaizhan. So the brick stayed on top of the pass. You didn't believe the story, but now you can't help wondering. You're tempted to touch the brick, but maybe you shouldn't in case the story really is true.

To ignore the brick and move onto the next project, turn to page 86.

To touch the brick, turn to page 98.

As you wonder where to go next, you overhear two workers talking. They mention that Qi Jiguang wants more beacon towers for better communication along the wall. You think think working on the beacon towers would be a good job for you.

The thousands of soldiers stationed on the wall must communicate with one another. They have to send warnings of enemy attacks and other important information. But the wall stretches over large distances of rough and rocky land. Messengers on horseback are too slow. So soldiers communicate with signals. During the day they use smoke signals. At night they use fire signals. Soldiers send signals from all of the towers, but the beacon towers are specially made for communication.

There are already hundreds of beacon towers along the wall, but most of them are earthen platforms. Qi Jiguang wants more. You have ideas for several kinds of beacon towers. Some towers will be built on the wall. Some will be in enemy lands just outside of the wall. This way they can be seen across a wider distance. The beacon towers must be close together so they are in view of one another. If mountains are in the way, the towers must be even closer together.

Qi Jiguang is pleased with your designs. "Messages can go fast along the beacon towers on the wall," he says. "That will allow the soldiers to move quickly against the enemy." He likes the towers outside the walls, but he doesn't want them to be too far away. "We do not want the soldiers stationed on those walls to feel isolated," he says. "They might be afraid to shoot an arrow!"

To scout a location for a tower outside the wall, turn to page 80.

To begin construction on a beacon tower on the wall, turn to page 82.

You spend several days looking for a good spot to build a beacon tower. The area must be level, which is hard to find in this mountainous place. Finally you find the perfect spot. It is wide enough for a tower, and within sight of the wall.

The process of sending smoke signals from beacon towers was a central part of the Great Wall defensive systems.

Qi Jiguang gives you a construction crew made up of soldiers. Your crew gets to work right away. After gathering plenty of stone and earth, they begin building the beacon tower.

Some beacon towers are round, but this one is square. The tower goes up quickly. The bottom floor is designed as a stable for sheep and horses. The second floor will be an area for sleeping. The soldiers build a large furnace on the top of the tower. The beacon fires will be lit in the furnace.

To return to the wall and begin construction on another tower, turn to page 82.

To search for fuel for the furnace, turn to page 97.

You head back to the wall. Before long you have begun work on a new tower. The beacon towers are narrow and square, with two furnaces on the top. If an enemy is sighted, the soldiers light a fire in the tower. The crew on the next tower will see it and light a fire. The next crew will see that fire, and so on until everyone sees the signals. Every morning and evening each signal crew sends an "all clear" signal. If one tower misses sending the "all clear," it means that tower is under attack. Soldiers can also use cannons to signal the other tower crews.

As the soldiers work on the tower, one of them asks you, "Have you ever heard the saying, 'a single smile costs one thousand pieces of gold?'" You shake your head.

"Once there was an Empress who never smiled," he says. "The emperor offered a reward to anyone who could make the empress smile. One of the court officials told the emperor to set a fire in a beacon tower to fool the army. So the emperor had a beacon fire lit. The army rushed to the emperor, who laughed at their mistake. The empress laughed too! The soldiers were angry that they had marched all the way down the mountain.

"The emperor loved the joke so much that he did it many times. Finally the soldiers stopped believing the emperor. One day enemies really attacked. But when the emperor lit the beacon fire, no one came. The enemies killed the emperor and took the empress prisoner."

Turn the page.

Soon this tower is finished and you move on.
In a few weeks many new beacon towers have been
built on the wall. Qi Jiguang praises your good work.

Some beacon tower communications included
cannon fire and drums in addition to traditional
smoke and fire signals. Chinese troops on the wall
tried to find the best way to send clear information
about approaching enemy invaders.

One evening you are enjoying the sunset over the mountains when you see a signal fire on a nearby beacon tower. They must be under attack! You watch the beacon tower carefully. One signal means there are ferwer than 20 Mongols in the raiding party. Two signals means there could be as many as 100 Mongols. Finally you see a second signal. You look around for the soldiers who have the job of lighting the fire, but they're nowhere to be seen. You want to join in the fight against the Mongols, but someone must light the signal fire quickly.

To attack the Mongols, turn to page 88.

To light the signal fire, turn to page 90.

It's just an old brick. But you can't bring yourself to touch it. Quickly you finish the repairs and move on to another area. Walls, gates, and towers need your attention.

The months wear on. You're lonely for your family, and the few letters you get now and then are not enough. Qi Jiguang sends word that you are to stay at the pass until everything is done. He writes that he will send you something special to help the job go faster.

One day you are out making repairs when shouts ring out from the main gate. It is your family! Qi Jiguang must have sent for them. He sometimes gives soldiers permission to bring their families along. You are grateful and overjoyed to have your family with you. Qi Jiguang was right—your work will go much faster now.

THE END

To follow another path, turn to page 11.
To read the conclusion, turn to page 101.

You always wanted to be in the army, and you're sure someone else will light the fire. You grab a spear and scramble down the tower. Soldiers are already fighting the Mongols, and you join in. You attack several Mongols with your spear before you are hit with an arrow. Crawling slowly over blood-soaked bodies to a nearby tree, you pass out.

Despite the advantages provided by the wall, some invaders were able to penetrate its defenses.

Some time later a sharp pain awakens you. A Chinese soldier is pulling the arrow out of your shoulder. He bandages the wound and carries you back to the barracks. After many weeks the wound heals, but you will never be able to use your arm again. Your career as a builder and architect is over.

THE END

To follow another path, turn to page 11.
To read the conclusion, turn to page 101.

Quickly you climb up the ladder to the top of the beacon tower. You realize that the tower soldiers were one step ahead of you. They saw the signal too, and they are already preparing to light the beacon fire. You help pile leaves, wood, and animal dung into each furnace and light the piles. Soon you see two fires in the tower farther down the wall. In only a few minutes, every tower you can see has lit their signals.

The soldiers rush to attack the Mongols, but you stay on the tower. You want to fight, but after seeing the fearsome Mongol warriors you realize you need more battle training first. Shouting and the clash of weapons fills the air. Suddenly a stray arrow whizzes through the air. It hits you in the chest, ending your career as a respected architect of the Great Wall.

THE END

To follow another path, turn to page 11.
To read the conclusion, turn to page 101.

You politely decline the offer. Qi Jiguang says nothing, but it's clear he is not happy. He doesn't say anything more about it, and you go on with your work. Slowly the towers go up. Some of them are a half mile apart. Others can be up to 2 miles apart. It depends on how steep and rough the land is. All of the towers must be within sight of one another.

The Ming Dynasty lasted from AD 1368 to 1644. Ming rulers constantly strengthened and maintained the Great Wall with the hope of preventing invasions.

One day Qi Jiguang appears. "Your work here is done," he says abruptly. The last towers are not finished, but you understand. He is sending you home in disgrace. Quickly you pack your belongings and leave. Qi Jiguang will probably make sure you never work as a designer again. Even the idea of seeing your family doesn't help ease the bitterness.

THE END

To follow another path, turn to page 11.
To read the conclusion, turn to page 101.

Solid towers are made of earth and are much easier to build than the hollow ones. Workers build up the earthen towers, and then the tops are paved with bricks to make a platform. The soldiers use the towers for watching the fighting and for attacking enemies. The soldiers don't like the solid towers, though. It is hard to get up onto the top of a solid tower. The only way to do it is to climb a rope up the side. If the enemy attacks, the soldiers near solid towers don't have anywhere to hide. But you insist on building some, because they are good for signaling.

One day you are on top of a solid tower, overseeing the bricklayers. It's a clear day and you can see a group of riders approach the tower. It takes you a moment to realize that they are not Chinese soldiers. They are Mongol invaders! Before you can move, an arrow flies upward, hitting you in the chest. As your blood stains the newly laid bricks, you become another victim of Mongol attackers.

THE END

To follow another path, turn to page 11.
To read the conclusion, turn to page 101.

Fighting soldiers must be protected from the enemy's arrows, but they also have to be able to fire down at the enemy. The tower walls look like dragon's teeth, with open sections for the archers. Some of the walls have small holes that soldiers can use to drop rocks on enemies. Every tower in the area will have this design for the battlements. Qi Jiguang orders you to stay and oversee them all.

You had hoped you could return to your family soon, but now that is impossible. Qi Jiguang sees your sadness. "Go home and see your family, then come back to finish your work," he says. Soon you are on the road home, excited to see your family. You are also glad that you can return to the wall to see it finished.

THE END

To follow another path, turn to page 11.
To read the conclusion, turn to page 101.

The fires need fuel, so you take a crew to search the area for things to burn. You find plenty of wood, grass, and reeds. Sometimes you come across animal dung, which is also a good fuel. You have heard that wolf dung is the best, but you don't find any of that.

It's time to test the new furnace. Soldiers use ropes and buckets to get the fuel to the top of the tower. You climb the narrow ladder to the top of the tower too. It's windy, but you give the order to light the fire anyway. A gust of wind blows the fire toward you, and you take a step back. You're closer to the edge than you had realized. You tumble off the edge and die on the rocky ground far below.

THE END

To follow another path, turn to page 11.
To read the conclusion, turn to page 101.

You don't believe in old superstitions, so you move the brick to finish the repairs. As you begin to climb down the ladder, something moves beneath you. The ladder wobbles and then crashes to the ground along with you. You spend many weeks recovering from your injuries. Even when you heal, you can never work again. Did moving the brick make the tower move? That question gnaws at you for the rest of your life.

THE END

To follow another path, turn to page 11.
To read the conclusion, turn to page 101.

The Great Wall has a huge number of sections stretched over many types of terrain. This has made it difficult to determine the wall's exact length.

An early image of the Great Wall taken by British photographer Herbert Ponting in 1907.

CHAPTER 5

BEYOND THE GREAT WALL

People used to think that you could see the Great Wall of China from space. You can't easily see the wall from space, but the Great Wall has other claims to fame. It is one of the largest manmade objects on Earth. It is the longest wall in the world. The wall stretches across parts of China for more than 2,000 miles, with another 2,195 miles of branches and extra sections. Today it is considered one of the wonders of the world.

Many people think that the Great Wall is one long wall that stretches across China. But the Great Wall is really many pieces of long, disconnected walls. The first long wall went up during the reign of the First Emperor, Qin Shi Huang. He ruled China for only 15 years (221–206 BC) before his death. Qin Shi Huang's general, Meng Tian, died soon after.

For the next 500 years, emperors built and rebuilt the wall. Others ignored it. When the Ming Dynasty took control of China in 1368, the emperor was desperate to keep the Mongols out for good. The Ming era became the "golden age" of the Great Wall. Old earthen walls were repaired and new walls were built with stones and bricks. The wall became a strong military defense against the Mongols and other nomadic tribes. The Ming emperors built most of the Great Wall that exists today.

By the end of the Ming Dynasty, wars had changed. Cannons and gunpowder replaced arrows and spears. Battles were fought far from the Great Wall. The wall was no longer a great military fortress. It had become useless.

Slowly the wind and rain turned the strong wall into ruins. In some areas the wall disappeared completely. Local farmers pried the bricks and stones out of the walls and used them to build houses and roads.

Many Chinese forgot the Great Wall. The rest of the world barely knew it existed at all. Few foreigners saw the wall until the mid-1900s. China began allowing foreign visitors into the country in the 1970s. The Great Wall and its long, sometimes sad history became well known to Americans when U.S. President Richard Nixon visited it in 1972.

In 1987 the Great Wall was added to the list of World Heritage Sites. It was honored as "one of the world's great feats of engineering and an enduring monument to the strength of an ancient civilization."

Today many sections of the wall have been restored. Tourists from around the world come to climb its steep steps. In other places the wall is still in ruins, waiting to be rebuilt. The Great Wall stands as a symbol of China's strength and greatness.

Restoration projects have helped to preserve some parts of the Great Wall.

TIMELINE

800–221 BC—Chinese federal states build walls and fortifications around their territories.

221 BC—Qin Shi Huang unifies the warring states to become First Emperor of China.

221–209 BC—The First Emperor gives the order that new defensive walls be built around his empire.

209 BC—The First Emperor dies; the Han Dynasty begins.

130–102 BC—The Han Dynasty repairs parts of the wall and adds some walls in the eastern and western parts of China.

AD 423–1368—Various emperors repair, rebuild, and add sections to the wall.

1368—The Ming Dynasty begins.

1368–1644—Towers, battlements, passes, forts, and garrisons are built along the Great Wall. The wall is extended for hundreds of miles.

1644—The Ming Dynasty ends and the Great Wall begins its fall into ruins.

1923—The first claim is made that the Great Wall can be seen from space.

1950s—With the encouragment of the Chinese government, parts of the Great Wall are demolished. The bricks are used for building houses, farms, and other structures.

1987—The Great Wall becomes a World Heritage Site. World Heritage Sites are named to recognize cultural and natural places that have outstanding universal value.

2002—The Great Wall is designated as one of the world's most endangered sites.

2003—The Chinese government announces a series of new regulations and laws to better protect and preserve the Great Wall.

OTHER PATHS TO EXPLORE

In this book you've seen how the events of the past look different from three points of view. Perspectives on history are as varied as the people who lived it. Seeing history from many points of view is an important part of understanding it. Here are some ideas for other Great Wall of China points of view to explore:

- Many people died building the Great Wall of China, though no one knows the exact number. The construction took place over many centuries. Consider the time and labor it took to construct the Great Wall and compare the process to modern engineering projects such as China's Three Gorges Dam. How do they compare? Support your answer with examples from the text and other sources. (Integration of Knowledge and Ideas)

- Soldiers hated to be stationed on the Great Wall. It was in the middle of nowhere. They were separated from friends and family for months or years at a time. The soldiers didn't get much food or supplies. Every day there was the threat of attack. Discuss some of the reasons some soldiers might not accept this life, while others might stay loyal to the military. Support your answer with examples from the text and other sources. (Key Ideas and Details)

READ MORE

Collins, Terry. *Ancient China: An Interactive History Adventure.* Mankato, Minn.: Capstone Press, 2013.

Coupe, Robert. *The Great Wall of China.* New York: PowerKids Press, 2013.

Deady, Kathleen W., and Muriel L. Dubois. *Ancient China: Beyond the Great Wall.* Mankato, Minn.: Capstone Press, 2011.

INTERNET SITES

FactHound offers a safe, fun way to find Internet sites related to this book. All of the sites on FactHound have been researched by our staff.

Here's all you do:

Visit *www.facthound.com*

Type in this code: 9781491403990

GLOSSARY

architect (AR-ki-tekt)—a person who designs buildings and structures and advises in their construction

bandit (BAN-dit)—a robber or outlaw

battlement (BAT-uhl-muhnt)—a defensive wall with open areas to shoot through

beacon (BEE-kuhn)—a signal that is sometimes used as a warning

clay (KLAY)—a thick, sticky material from wet earth that can be molded and baked until hard

dung (DUHNG)—solid waste from animals

garrison (GA-ruh-suhn)—a place where troops are stationed

kiln (KILN)—a hot oven or chamber used to fire clay

nomad (NOH-mad)—a person who moves from place to place to find food and water, rather than living in one spot

peasant (PEZ-uhnt)—a poor person who owns a small farm or works on a farm

BIBLIOGRAPHY

Duiker, William J., and Jackson J. Spielvogel. *The Essential World History.* Boston: Wadsworth, Cengage Learning, 2013.

Ebrey, Patricia Buckley. *The Cambridge Illustrated History of China.* Cambridge, New York: Cambridge University Press, 2010.

Graff, David A., and Robin Higham. *A Military History of China.* Lexington, Ky.: University Press of Kentucky, 2012.

Keay, John. *China: A History.* New York: Basic Books, a member of the Perseus Books Group, 2009.

Loewe, Michael. *Everyday Life in Early Imperial China: During the Han Period, 202 BC–AD 220.* Indianapolis: Hackett Pub. Co., 2005.

Ong, Siew Chey. *China Condensed: 5,000 Years of History & Culture.* Singapore: Times Editions Marshall Cavendish, 2005.

Sterling, Brent L. *Do Good Fences Make Good Neighbors?: What History Teaches Us about Strategic Barriers and International Security.* Washington, D.C.: Georgetown University Press, 2009.

Wright, David Curtis. *The History of China.* Santa Barbara, Calif.: Greenwood, 2011.

INDEX